Climbing

She is up
on the gate.

She is up
on the wall.

She is up
on the fort.

She is up
on the slide.

She is up
on the swing.

She is up
on the stool.

She is up
on the ladder.

She is up
on the bunk.